THEODORE ROOSEVELT

ENCYCLOPEDIA
of PRESIDENTS

Theodore Roosevelt

Twenty-Sixth President of the United States

By Zachary Kent

Consultant: Charles Abele, Ph.D.
Social Studies Instructor
Chicago Public School System

CHILDRENS PRESS ®

CHICAGO

**President Roosevelt in the doorway of West Creek Ranch
House in Colorado with his dog Skip on his lap, April 1905**

Library of Congress Cataloging-in-Publication Data

Kent, Zachary.
  Theodore Roosevelt / by Zachary Kent.
    p.   cm. — (Encyclopedia of presidents)
  Includes index.
  Summary: Examines the personality, early life, family, and
career of the twenty-sixth president of the United States.
  ISBN 0-516-01354-8
  1. Roosevelt, Theodore, 1858-1919—Juvenile
literature. 2. Presidents—United States—Biography—
Juvenile literature. [1. Roosevelt, Theodore, 1858-
1919. 2. Presidents.] I. Title. II. Series.
E757.K33 1988   87-35184
973.91'1'0924—dc19   CIP
[B]   AC
[92]

Picture Acknowledgments

AP/Wide World Photos—4, 17, 19 (top), 26, 31,
35 (left), 39, 42, 49, 50, 53, 63 (2 photos), 73,
80, 85, 87

The Bettmann Archive, Inc.—6, 9, 11, 19
(bottom), 21 (right), 30, 32, 33, 35 (right), 40,
45 (bottom), 55, 61, 67, 69 (bottom), 71, 74, 88

Courtesy Library of Congress—21 (left), 28, 56,
58

Nawrocki Stock Photo—36, 45 (top), 69 (top),
79

Courtesy Sagamore Hill National Historic Site—
12, 14 (2 photos), 24, 25, 54 (bottom), 72, 76,
78, 82

UPI/Bettmann Newsphotos—5, 54 (top), 64, 89

U.S. Bureau of Printing and Engraving—2

Courtesy U.S. Department of the Army—47

Cover design and illustration by
Steven Gaston Dobson

Roosevelt in 1914 after his trip to Brazil

Table of Contents

Chapter 1

"Get Action!"

Bullets tore through the humid Cuban air and ripped the dense jungle grass. From the crest of two high hills, entrenched Spanish soldiers poured a withering gunfire down upon their American enemy. Troops of the First U.S. Volunteer Cavalry Regiment crouched along a shallow creek bank seeking protection. Dressed in blue flannel shirts and khaki trousers, some of these "Rough Riders" clutched at wounds and screamed in pain. Others sweated and fainted under the broiling tropical sun. As the minutes passed during the morning of July 1, 1898, the ranks thinned. But these men had come to Cuba to fight, and anxiously they awaited orders.

Most impatient of all was the regiment's commander, a brawny thirty-nine-year-old, easily recognized by his pince-nez glasses, gritted teeth, and thick moustache. When the United States declared war on Spain in April 1898, Theodore Roosevelt promptly resigned his post as assistant secretary of the navy. Forming an unusual volunteer regiment filled with hardy western cowboys and Indians, as well as refined Ivy League college graduates, Lieutenant Colonel Roosevelt had vowed to help the Cubans in their war of independence.

Opposite page: Roosevelt in his Rough Rider uniform

At last an officer brought Roosevelt a welcome message: "Move forward and support the regulars in the assault on the hills in front." Galloping along before his troops, he quickly formed them into battle line. "Are you afraid to stand up when I am on horseback?" he yelled at one hesitant soldier. A bullet, most likely aimed at Roosevelt, struck the man dead before he could respond.

Forced to leave their horses behind in Florida, the enlisted Rough Riders marched forward on foot. Riding back and forth, Colonel Roosevelt shouted words of encouragement. When they reached the foot of the first rise, later named Kettle Hill, the Rough Riders came upon several regiments of regular U.S. troops. A captain there stated that his men could not advance without proper orders, and that his colonel was nowhere in sight.

"Then I am the ranking officer here," commanded Roosevelt, "and I give the order to charge."

The captain remained reluctant until Roosevelt next said, "Then let my men through, sir." Excited regular soldiers jumped up and joined the charge. "The whole line," Roosevelt recalled, "tired of waiting, and eager to close with the enemy, was straining to go forward." Out of the cover of the woods and up the grassy slope these blue-jackets surged, shouting and firing as they ran.

Two black soldiers of a "colored" regiment threw down a fence so Roosevelt could ride ahead. Watching from a distance, newspaperman Richard Harding Davis later wrote that "Roosevelt mounted high on horseback, and charging the rifle-pits at a gallop and quite alone, made you feel that you would like to cheer."

Colonel Roosevelt (fourth from right) and his Rough Riders

Being on horseback, Roosevelt was able to advance well ahead of his foot soldiers. A bullet grazed his elbow. Near the summit he sprang from his horse and climbed over a barbed wire fence. Joining their colonel, the Rough Riders rushed for the crest of Kettle Hill in the face of enemy fire, until the Spaniards threw down their guns and ran.

The Rough Riders shouted for joy and cheered in victory. To the left, Roosevelt spied other U.S. troops storming the forts on neighboring San Juan Hill. "Obviously," the colonel remembered, "the proper thing to do was to help them. . . ." In another few minutes Roosevelt excitedly shouted for his troops to join in the charge on San Juan Hill. Thinking that the men would all come, he recalled, "I jumped over the wire fence in front of us and started at the double. . . . After running about a hundred yards I found I had only five men along with me."

As bullets whizzed around him, Roosevelt ran back up Kettle Hill. "We didn't hear you, we didn't see you go, Colonel," honestly exclaimed his surprised soldiers. "Lead on now," they promised, "we'll sure follow you." Together with the black troopers of the Ninth Regiment, the soldiers of the First, and others, the Rough Riders followed Roosevelt and swarmed up San Juan Hill. The overpowered Spaniards jumped up from their trenches. With his revolver, Roosevelt shot one dead. Driving the enemy from the ridge, the Americans chased them until they neared the important city of Santiago.

During the next few days the U.S. Army fought off repeated Spanish counterattacks, while the U.S. Navy destroyed the Spanish fleet trapped in Santiago harbor. By the middle of July the war in Cuba was over.

"Oh, but we have had a bully fight!" Roosevelt joyfully exclaimed. News of his valiant charge soon electrified the United States and made the colonel famous. Americans seeking to learn more about Roosevelt discovered he was a man of many talents. Secretary of State John Hay truthfully described him as being a man "of gentle birth and breeding, yet a man of the people . . . with the training of a scholar and the breezy accessibility of a ranchman; a man of the library and a man of the world; an athlete and a thinker; a soldier and a statesman . . . with the sensibility of a poet and the steel nerve of a rough rider."

Above all, America's new folk hero was a man of incredible energy. Popularly elected vice-president in 1900, Roosevelt became the twenty-sixth United States president upon the death of President William McKinley

The Rough Riders atop San Juan Hill

the next year. With vigor Roosevelt entered the White House and seemed almost single-handedly to sweep away the cobwebs of the 1800s and propel the nation forward into the twentieth century. "Get action," Roosevelt demanded of the American people, "do things; be sane; don't fritter away your time; create, act, take a place wherever you are and be somebody!" Charging through life, the same way he charged up San Juan Hill, Theodore Roosevelt always got action.

Chapter 2

A Fighter Is Born

On October 27, 1858, servants scurried from the Roosevelt house at 28 East 20th Street in New York City in search of doctors, midwives, and family relatives. At a quarter to eight that night Theodore Roosevelt, Jr. was born, "as sweet and pretty a young baby as I have ever seen," announced his grandmother. Nicknamed "Teedie," the boy was the son of a millionaire, Theodore Roosevelt, Sr., who worked as a banker and importer of glass. In his spare time he organized and supported many city charities. "My father," Roosevelt later wrote, ". . . was the best man I ever knew. He combined strength and courage with gentleness, tenderness, and great unselfishness." Young Theodore's mother, Martha Bulloch Roosevelt, was a Georgia belle. "My mother," he remembered, "was a sweet, gracious, beautiful Southern woman, a delightful companion, and beloved by everybody."

As a child, Theodore was frail and sickly. He suffered severe bouts of asthma that made it difficult for him to breathe. Some nights his choking spells made it necessary for him to sleep propped up in bed or sitting in a chair. At other times his father bundled him up and took him for fast carriage rides. Speeding down the streets, these rides forced air into Teedie's weak lungs.

Opposite page: "Teedie" at four years of age   13

Theodore's parents, Theodore, Sr. and Martha

As Theodore was too ill to attend school, his aunt, Annie
Bulloch, tutored him at home. At his bedside Aunt Annie
and his mother told him stories of Daniel Boone and Davy
Crockett and tales of Southern folklore. The wealthy
Roosevelts owned a large library of books. Curled up in a
favorite chair, Teedie excitedly pored through history
books and novels. "I was nervous and timid," remembered
Roosevelt of his early childhood. "Yet from reading of the
people I admired—ranging from the soldiers of Valley
Forge, and Morgan's riflemen, to the heroes of my favorite
stories . . . I felt a great admiration for men who were
fearless . . . and I had a great desire to be like them."

In the summers Theodore's father took the family on vacations in the country. As often as possible Teedie joined his two sisters and his brother outside. For fun the Roosevelt children went "picking apples, hunting frogs . . . gathering hickory-nuts and chestnuts . . . building wigwams in the woods, and sometimes playing Indians. . . ."

Skinny and coughing, still Teedie never tired of inventing games and adventures to play. Sometimes little Edith Carow, a family friend three years younger than Teedie, also took part in the fun.

At the age of seven Theodore developed a serious interest in zoology. Walking near his home one day, he spotted a dead seal laid out in a Broadway marketplace. The animal, killed in the harbor, excited the boy's imagination.

"As long as that seal remained there," he later declared, "I haunted the neighborhood of the market day after day." He took measurements with a ruler and recorded guesses about the seal's strength. Somehow obtaining the seal's skull, he started in his bedroom the "Roosevelt Museum of Natural History."

Eager to learn, the young scientist snared all kinds of animals and preserved them for study. As a nine-year-old, his growing collection of insects inspired him to prepare a "Natural History on Insects." "All the insects that I write about in this book," he explained, "inhabbit [sic] North America. Now and then a friend has told me something about them but mostly I have gained their habbits [sic] from ofserv-a-tion [sic]."

The Roosevelts encouraged their son in his quest for knowledge. Because he was still thin and weak, however, they worried about his health. When he reached ten, his father took him aside. "Theodore, you have the mind but you have not the body. . . . You must *make* your body."

Through clenched teeth the boy immediately vowed: *"I'll make my body."*

Determined to build his strength, Theodore spent hours at Woods' Gymnasium in the neighborhood. On the second floor porch of the family brownstone, his father also installed athletic equipment for his son. Day after day the boy lifted barbells, swung chest weights, and exercised on parallel bars. He also took boxing lessons.

To enable Theodore to shoot birds for his wildlife collection, his father presented him with his first gun in the summer of 1872. Poor marksmanship and an inability to read distant billboards revealed his nearsightedness. "I spoke of this to my father," he recounted, "and soon afterwards got my first pair of spectacles. . . . I had no idea how beautiful the world was until I got those spectacles."

Partly for Theodore's health, the entire Roosevelt family sailed across the Atlantic in 1869 and again in 1872, for extensive trips in Europe and the Middle East. Traveling in comfort, Theodore spent a Christmas in Rome, boated on the Nile River in Egypt, and climbed the Pyramids. In Dresden, Germany, he studied German and French during one summer. Greatly impressed by his thoughtfulness, his instructor, Fräulein Anna Minkwitz, predicted, "He will surely one day be a great professor, or who knows, he may become president of the United States."

Theodore at age seventeen

Squinting through his glasses and grinning with his big teeth, the growing teenager continued his studies in natural history. His parents, however, decided he must begin his formal education as preparation for Harvard College. At the family's new house at 6 West 57th Street, Mr. Arthur Cutler privately tutored fifteen-year-old Theodore in several subjects six to eight hours a day. He proved a wonderful, hard-working student. "The young man," recalled Cutler, "never seemed to know what idleness was." Even in his free time Theodore pored over books of literature and science. Soon he realized he possessed a photographic memory, enabling him to remember completely everything he read.

In the fall of 1876 the young man rented an apartment at 16 Winthrop Street in Cambridge, Massachusetts, and entered Harvard College as a freshman. Like a whirlwind he threw himself into his studies. "Never have I seen or read of a man with such an amazing array of interests," declared a classmate. With opinions on every subject, the eighteen-year-old never seemed afraid to speak his mind. In class he repeatedly jumped to his feet to interrupt lectures, until one professor complained, "See here, Roosevelt, let me talk. I'm running this course."

Popular among his rich classmates, Theodore received invitations to join several college clubs and societies. "It seems perfectly wonderful," he exclaimed in a letter to his mother, "looking back over my eighteen years of existence, to see how I have literally never spent an unhappy day, unless by my own fault." Grief finally overtook the young man, however, during his sophomore year when his father died of cancer. Deeply shaken by the loss, Theodore mourned, "How I wish I could do something to keep up his good name!"

Physical activity helped him forget his sadness. Standing five feet eight inches tall, the blue-eyed boy through years of exercise had molded his body into lean and muscular shape. Now through the summer of 1878 swimming, rowing, hiking, hunting, running, and horseback riding filled his hours at the family's vacation home at Oyster Bay, Long Island.

A boxing match during his junior year at Harvard revealed Theodore's gritty courage to his classmates. Boxing as a 135-pound lightweight, Roosevelt reached the

Above: Theodore and
fellow members of the
Porcelain Club of
Harvard University

Right: Theodore at
Harvard in his track
meet uniform

finals of the annual competition. As he stepped into the ring with the defending champion, C. S. Hanks, the two began to battle. With his poor eyesight and shorter reach, Theodore had little chance of winning the bout. One spectator exclaimed, "It was no fight at all. . . . You should have seen that little fellow staggering about, banging the air. Hanks couldn't put him out and Roosevelt wouldn't give up. It wasn't a fight, but, oh, he showed himself a fighter!"

Roosevelt showed the same kind of determination after he fell in love. In October 1878, classmate Richard Saltonstall took Theodore to visit his family's mansion on Boston's exclusive Chestnut Hill. There Theodore met Saltonstall's cousin, Alice Hathaway Lee. "As long as I live," Roosevelt later proclaimed, "I shall never forget how sweetly she looked, and how prettily she greeted me." Almost instantly Theodore decided "that win her I would if it were possible." Dressed in dandy clothes and wearing brushed sideburns, he called on her often and escorted her to dances. Only seventeen, however, and unwilling to commit herself, Alice often teased him. Still Theodore would not give up. At a party he pointed across the room and exclaimed to a friend, "See that girl? I am going to marry her. She won't have me, but I am going to have *her!*"

Gradually Theodore's charm and zest captured Alice Lee's heart and she agreed to marry him. In the spring of 1880 he graduated from Harvard with honors, ranking 21 in a class of 177. The following fall, on October 27, his twenty-second birthday, Roosevelt married nineteen-year-old Alice Lee in Brookline, Massachusetts.

Alice Hathaway Lee and Theodore after his Harvard graduation

Theodore and his young bride moved into the family home on West 57th Street in New York City. Encouraged by Alice, Roosevelt put aside his plans to become a natural scientist. Instead he entered Columbia Law School and considered starting a career as a politician. During spare hours he did historical research and with pen in hand labored on a book entitled *The Naval War of 1812*. When G. P. Putnam published the work in 1881, reviewers hailed it as the most important text ever written on the subject. Its success established twenty-three-year-old Roosevelt as a promising scholarly writer.

A grand honeymoon in the spring of 1881 gave Roosevelt a chance to show Alice the sights of Europe. Lovingly he claimed his wife to be "the best traveling companion I have ever known." In Switzerland the tireless young tourist took time to climb the craggy 15,000-foot peak of the Matterhorn.

Returning to New York, Roosevelt found his law studies dull. He much preferred to spend his time at Morton Hall, the local Republican Club. Roosevelt's wealthy friends frowned on local politics, claiming it was a dirty business that gentlemen avoided. "If this were so," responded Roosevelt, "it merely meant that the people I knew did not belong to the governing class . . . and that I intended to be one of the governing class."

At Morton Hall Roosevelt rubbed elbows with Irish saloonkeepers and other rough city politicians. One local leader, Joe Murray, soon took notice of Roosevelt's polished habits and keen intellect.

As the fall election for the district's state assemblyman neared, Murray approached him. "Mr. Roosevelt," he asked, ". . . will you take the nomination?" Hesitantly Roosevelt agreed to run.

Family and friends in the Twenty-First District rallied to Roosevelt's support. The *New York Times* called the honest young man "a public-spirited citizen" and a fellow "who should be sought for office." On election day, November 9, 1881, Roosevelt easily beat his Democratic opponent 3,490 votes to 1,989.

When he arrived at the New York State Assembly in Albany at the start of 1882, Roosevelt's fancy clothes and refined manners immediately made an impression. At one early meeting he burst into the room and Assemblyman John Walsh remembered, "Suddenly our eyes . . . became glued on a young man who was coming in through the door. His hair was parted in the center, and he had sideburns. He wore a single eye-glass, with a gold chain over his ear. . . . He carried a gold-headed cane in one hand, a silk hat in the other, and he walked in the bent-over fashion that was the style with the young men of the day. . . ."

"Who's the dude?" Walsh asked another member.

"That's Theodore Roosevelt of New York," the man answered.

As the lawmaking session began, Roosevelt often rose in the assembly to submit bills and offer opinions. His high-pitched voice and drawled Harvard accent calling out "Mr. Speak-ah! Mr. Speak-ah!" attracted amused notice. "We almost shouted with laughter," recalled Assemblyman Isaac Hunt of one occasion, but as Roosevelt kept talking, "our attention was drawn upon what he had to say because there was force in his remarks."

Legislators who admired Roosevelt's energetic style soon called him "the Cyclone Assemblyman." Newspapers praised his efforts to bring more honesty into the government, and he grew in popularity throughout the state. The next year, while still the youngest assemblyman in Albany, Republican members elected twenty-four-year-old Roosevelt to the post of minority leader. Recalling his early career, Roosevelt later declared, "I rose like a rocket."

Sitting on the steps of their parents' home in Oyster Bay are Theodore
(left) and brother Elliot. The three ladies (left to right) are sister Corinne,
wife Alice, and sister Anna.

His rapid political success suddenly seemed unimpor-
tant when Roosevelt suffered a double tragedy early in
1884. On February 12 he became the proud father of a
baby girl. Childbirth complications, however, caused his
wife to fall gravely ill. At the very same time, Roosevelt's
mother lay in bed, stricken with typhoid fever. Through
the early morning hours of February 14 Roosevelt watched
and prayed at the family brownstone. "There is a curse on
this house," he moaned when his mother died. Before the

Roosevelt (standing, right) with fellow New York assemblymen

day ended, his own darling Alice also died, a victim of kidney failure. Completely stunned by the loss of his wife, Roosevelt exclaimed, "When my heart's dearest died the light went from my life for ever."

Leaving his baby daughter, named Alice, in the care of his older sister, Roosevelt escaped west to the Badlands of the Dakota Territory. "He hiked away to the wilderness to get away from the world," Assemblyman Hunt recalled. "He went out there a broken-hearted man."

Chapter 3

The Four-Eyed Maverick

In the stark country of the Dakota Badlands, Roosevelt hoped to forget his personal sorrow. Using a large portion of his inheritance he purchased Chimney Butte and Elkhorn, two ranches along the Little Missouri River. He hired ranch hands, stocked his land with cattle, and built a log cabin. "I grow very fond of the place," he soon revealed. In the evenings he sat watching the streaming colors of sunset. "My days," he explained, "I spend generally alone, riding through the lonely rolling prairie and broken lands."

The grizzled cowboys of the Badlands at first regarded Roosevelt as a ridiculous eastern dude. "I now look like a regular cowboy dandy," even he admitted. "You would be amused to see me," he wrote a friend, "in my broad sombrero hat, fringed and beaded buckskin shirt, horse hide chaparajos or riding trousers, and cowhide boots, with . . . silver spurs."

Ranch hands often chuckled at his unusual accent and educated vocabulary. "Hasten forward quickly there!" he ordered two hardened cowboys one day in his high, piping voice. Although ranch hands often swore aloud with the ugliest language imaginable, Roosevelt's most common curse was to shout "By Godfrey!"

Opposite page: Roosevelt the cowboy

Roosevelt in 1885
in his hunting gear
in the Dakota Badlands

Joining in all the ranch activity, Roosevelt gradually earned the respect of his hired help and neighbors. With a lasso he roped steers and then branded them with hot irons. He chipped his shoulder and fractured an arm when thrown from bucking broncos. Galloping across the plain one night he and another cowboy stopped a stampede of a thousand head of cattle. Riding alone for days on horseback, he hunted bison, deer, and elk. Once a huge nine-foot grizzly bear charged at him from about eight yards away. "Doubtless my face was pretty white," he remembered, but he shot the beast right between the eyes.

Ranchmen impressed by Roosevelt's fearlessness and fairness elected him president of the local Stockman's Association and made him a deputy sheriff of Billings County. On March 24, 1886, three thieves stole a boat from the Elkhorn Ranch. With two ranch hands Roosevelt built a flat-bottomed scow and pursued the thieves down the icy Little Missouri River. On the morning of April 1 they ambushed the robbers while they camped. "We took them absolutely by surprise," crowed Deputy Sheriff Roosevelt. "We straightened up from behind the bank, covering them with our cocked rifles, while I shouted to them to hold up their hands." Instead of hanging the captured men on the spot, according to common western practice, Roosevelt marched them forty miles overland to the jail at Dickinson, where they were tried and sentenced.

For three years Roosevelt lived the life of a cowboy. The sun tanned his face and the hard work improved his health, swelling his body with muscle. In his free time he penned a popular memoir entitled *Hunting Trips of a Ranchman*. His many adventures made him a minor Badlands folk hero. The men who knew him never laughed at him now. "That four-eyed maverick," summed up one weathered cowhand, "has sand in his craw a-plenty."

In the fall of 1885 Roosevelt returned to New York City to spend time with his baby daughter. During his stay he met his childhood friend, Edith Carow, again. Roosevelt discovered that Edith had grown into an attractive and charming young woman. The two fell instantly in love, and he proposed. However, the young widower asked that the engagement be kept a secret for a year.

Edith Carow Roosevelt

Edith traveled to England in the autumn of 1886 and Roosevelt intended to follow after her. New York City Republicans, however, had not forgotten the popular assemblyman. Searching for a reform candidate to run for mayor, Republican leaders approached the "Cowboy of Dakota." With strong Democrat and Labor party candidates also running, Roosevelt realized his chances of winning were slim. Still he threw himself into the campaign with boundless energy. Working eighteen hours a day, he held press conferences, shook hands, signed autographs, and shouted rousing speeches.

Roosevelt when he was running for mayor of New York City

In spite of this hard work, on election day in November 1886 Theodore Roosevelt placed a distant third. "AM BADLY DEFEATED," he wired a friend, "WORSE EVEN THAN I FEARED." "Be happy, Mr. Roosevelt, be happy while you may," teased the magazine *Puck*, "you are not the timber of which Presidents are made."

Turning his back on New York, Roosevelt sailed to London. On December 2, 1886, the twenty-eight-year-old found true happiness when he married twenty-five-year-old Edith Carow at Saint George's Church. "You have no idea how sweet Edith is," he confided to his sister, Corinne. "I don't think even I had known how wonderfully *good* and unselfish she is."

Sagamore Hill, Roosevelt's summer home in Oyster Bay, Long Island

A terrible blizzard in 1887 destroyed Roosevelt's cattle herds and ruined his Badlands investment. Using the last of his inheritance, carpenters earlier had hammered together a huge, rambling summer home for Roosevelt in Oyster Bay, Long Island. He named the place Sagamore Hill after an Indian word meaning chieftain. Settling in here and in a New York townhouse, Roosevelt turned to writing to repair his finances. "Mind you," he remarked to a friend, "I'm a literary fellow, not a politician, nowadays." A biography of pioneer Missouri senator Thomas Hart Benton rolled off the presses that year. Roosevelt also soon turned out a biography of revolutionary patriot Gouverneur Morris and an important history called *The Winning of the West*. Before the end of his life Roosevelt would publish a total of thirty-eight books.

The Roosevelt family: Theodore is holding Archie; Edith is holding
Kermit and Ethel; and Theodore, Jr. and Alice are standing.

During the next few years Edith Roosevelt carefully
managed the money and raised a family. Together the
Roosevelts had four sons and a daughter. Joining Alice
Roosevelt, these children filled Sagamore Hill with shouts
and laughter. Roosevelt romped with his boys and girls at
every opportunity. One summer as Edith Roosevelt prepared to take the family to Sagamore Hill, a friend asked if
her husband intended to leave on vacation also. "For
Heaven's sake!" joked Mrs. Roosevelt. "Don't put it into
Theodore's head to go too; I should have another child to
think of."

"I shall probably never be in politics again," Roosevelt gloomily wrote during this time. In 1888, however, Americans elected Republican Benjamin Harrison president of the United States. In search of a civil service commissioner, Harrison offered Roosevelt the post. Though the job only paid $3,500 a year, Roosevelt grabbed the chance. Arriving in Washington in May 1889, he immediately put himself to work.

For many years, with every change of administration, loyal party members had been rewarded with government jobs. Many people objected to this "spoils system." They demanded that thousands of government positions be held by the best qualified applicants regardless of politics. As a result, Congress in 1883 enacted the Civil Service Act. Now Commissioner Roosevelt, as a national watchdog, undertook the duty to see that job seekers fairly passed tests and obtained their federal positions on merit. Pacing his office and dictating letters, Roosevelt insisted that "the law should be enforced up the handle *everywhere*, fearlessly and honestly."

For four years Roosevelt fought government leaders who tried to fill federal jobs with unqualified friends. He uncovered cheating on tests and he exposed bribery. He especially attacked the tricky practices of Postmaster General John Wanamaker in handing out post office jobs. Astonished by his commissioner's activity, President Harrison finally remarked, "he wanted to put an end to all the evil in the world between sunrise and sunset."

When Democrat Grover Cleveland won the presidential election of 1892, he complimented Roosevelt. He asked the

Presidents Grover Cleveland (left) and Benjamin Harrison (right)

young Republican reformer to remain as civil service commissioner. For another two years Roosevelt hounded government spoilsmen. During spare hours he visited the local Cosmos Club, a friendly place where Washington scientists gathered to exchange ideas. One night British author Rudyard Kipling dropped by and heard Roosevelt pouring out detailed knowledge on all manner of subjects and discussing endless projects. "I curled up in the seat opposite," remembered Kipling, "and listened and wondered, until the universe seemed to be going round, and Theodore was the spinner."

Chapter 4

From Police Department to Navy Department

"Where are our offices? Where is the Board Room? Now what do we do?" enthusiastically boomed thirty-six-year-old Theodore Roosevelt as he strode into the Mulberry Street headquarters of the New York City Police Department. Restless in Washington, Roosevelt accepted Mayor William Strong's appointment in the spring of 1895 as a New York City police commissioner. Promptly elected president of the board of commissioners, Roosevelt vowed to root out corruption and laziness from the city police force.

Soon the *New York World* trumpeted, "We have a real police commissioner. . . . His teeth are big and white, his eyes are small and piercing. . . . His heart is full of reform . . . [and] he does look like a determined man." Within days Commissioner Roosevelt forced the resignation of the chief of police, whom he accused of taking bribes. Other dishonest officers quickly followed. One newspaper printed the headline "ROOSEVELT AS JUDGE—The Reform Commissioner Tries Nearly 100 Policemen in One Day." A reporter witnessing one trial exclaimed, "When he asks a question, Mr. Roosevelt shoots it at the poor trembling policeman as he would shoot a bullet at a coyote."

Opposite page: Roosevelt in 1895

At night common patrolmen, and the roundsmen sent to check up on them, sometimes failed to do their duty. In the darkness of June 7, 1895, Roosevelt stalked about the east side of Manhattan and caught six men loafing on the job. "ROOSEVELT AS ROUNDSMAN," happily proclaimed one newspaper. "Policemen Didn't Dream the President of the Board Was Catching Them Sleeping," another headline read.

On subsequent nights Roosevelt disguised himself with a black cape and a dark felt hat and prowled the streets in search of other misbehaving officers. "These midnight rambles are great fun," the hardy commissioner declared. "My whole work brings me in contact with every class of people in New York. . . . I get a glimpse of the real life of the swarming millions."

New York citizens cheered Roosevelt's colorful exploits, as nervous policemen stepped up their patrols and city streets grew safer. Roosevelt's enormous popularity lasted until he decided to enforce the city's Sunday Excise Law. This law forbade saloons from selling liquor on Sundays. For years, bribed policemen had looked the other way and had failed to close saloons. Now, however, Roosevelt insisted, "It is the plain duty of a public officer to stand steadfastly for the honest enforcement of the law." Throughout the summer of 1895, heavy fines and padlocked doors kept New Yorkers from their Sunday steins of beer. While many people complained, still others admired Roosevelt's integrity and high principles. In either case, Theodore Roosevelt's activities as New York City police commissioner were talked about across the entire country.

Roosevelt (center) as police commissioner of New York City

In 1896 Roosevelt toured the nation, giving rousing stump speeches on behalf of Republican presidential candidate William McKinley. After McKinley's election, the new president made Roosevelt assistant secretary of the navy. Ever since childhood Roosevelt had loved ships and the navy. Excitedly he arrived in Washington in the spring of 1897 to take up his new duties.

"Best man for the job," noted Secretary of the Navy John D. Long after first meeting Roosevelt. The assistant secretary threw himself into his work with customary energy. "He is full of suggestions," remarked Secretary Long, "many of which are of great value, and his spirit and forceful habit is a good tonic; but the very devil seems to possess him."

Roosevelt as assistant secretary of the navy

Fiercely patriotic, Roosevelt desired to see America build a modern navy. He called for more ships, better weapons, and sailors prepared to fight. On the Caribbean island of Cuba, revolutionaries were waging a war of independence against Spain. Roosevelt and many others believed the United States should join in this conflict.

During Secretary Long's vacations Roosevelt became acting secretary. Of one occasion he gleefully wrote a friend, "The Secretary is away and I am having immense fun running the navy." "The liveliest spot in Washington at present," reported the August 23, 1897, edition of the *New York Sun*, "is the Navy Department. The decks are cleared for action. Acting Secretary Roosevelt . . . has the whole Navy bordering on a war footing. It remains only to sand down the decks and pipe to quarters for action."

Slowly the United States drifted toward war. To protect the lives of American residents in Cuba, President McKinley sent the U.S. battleship *Maine* to Havana. On February 15, 1898, a mysterious explosion rocked the *Maine* and sent it to the bottom of the harbor. "The *Maine*," declared Roosevelt, "was sunk by an act of dirty treachery on the part of the Spaniards I believe." Angered Americans took to chanting "Remember the *Maine!*"

Still President McKinley resisted plunging the United States into a bloody war. Ferociously Roosevelt complained that McKinley had "the backbone of a chocolate eclair." When Secretary Long left the office for a few hours on the afternoon of February 25, Acting Secretary Roosevelt acted swiftly. He ordered Commodore George Dewey's American Pacific Fleet to Hong Kong to guard against the Spanish fleet in the Philippine Islands. He instructed other squadron commanders to "keep full of coal" and be ready to steam their ships into combat at a moment's notice. On returning to the office, Secretary Long declared with unhappy astonishment, "He has gone at things like a bull in a china shop."

Roosevelt remained proud of his accomplishments. "We will have this war for the freedom of Cuba," he loudly predicted in a public speech, "in spite of . . . timidity." Aroused by sensational newspaper stories printed in Joseph Pulitzer's *New York World* and William Randolph Hearst's *New York Journal*, millions of other Americans also demanded war. Finally President McKinley caved in to the public pressure, and on April 19, 1898, the United States declared war against Spain.

Chapter 5

Rough Rider
to the White House

"Theodore Roosevelt," wrote Secretary of State John Hay in surprise, ". . . has left the Navy Department where he had the chance of his life and has joined a cowboy regiment." Wildly eager to fight, in May 1898 Roosevelt resigned his government position and accepted a commission as a lieutenant colonel in the volunteer army. The War Department had announced that three new regiments would be "composed exclusively of frontiersmen possessing special qualifications as horsemen and marksmen." Roosevelt gladly agreed to organize the First U.S. Volunteer Cavalry Regiment, to be commanded by his friend Colonel Leonard Wood.

Applications arrived by the bushel, and Roosevelt carefully chose the men he wished to fight with him. "We had a number of first-class young fellows from the East," explained the lieutenant colonel, "most of them from colleges like Harvard, Yale, and Princeton; but the great majority of the men were Southwesterners, from the then territories of Oklahoma, Indian Territory, Arizona, and New Mexico. They . . . possessed hardihood and endurance . . . and, above all, they had the fighting edge."

Newspapers suggested such names for the unusual regiment as "Teddy's Terrors" and "Teddy's Riotous Rounders." Soon the name "Roosevelt's Rough Riders" stuck. Quickly the recruits gathered at Camp Wood in San Antonio, Texas, for their training. Ivy League quarterbacks, tennis champions, and polo players practiced riding, shooting, and marching alongside lean cowboys and sharpshooting Cherokees. In the evenings a camp band blared, "There'll be a Hot Time in the Old Town Tonight," and soon the army adopted the tune as the war's theme song.

By the end of May, Colonel Wood and Lieutenant Colonel Roosevelt had whipped the regiment into fighting shape. "In all the world," Roosevelt proudly wrote to President McKinley, "there is not a regiment I would so soon belong to." On May 1, 1898, Commodore George Dewey had steamed into Manila Bay in the Philippines and had destroyed the Spanish Asiatic Squadron. Now Roosevelt worried that the war would be over before his men had a chance to fight. With extra pairs of glasses packed in his baggage and sewn into the lining of his hat, Roosevelt hurried his troops aboard transport trains to Florida. At Tampa the soldiers joined the rest of the American invasion force loading onto ships. The commanding general, however, reduced the Rough Rider regiment to 560 men and ordered their horses left behind.

After several sweltering days aboard ship, the army reached the coast of Cuba on June 22. The troops disembarked at the village of Daiquiri. Eighteen miles to the north lay the city of Santiago.

Right: Cover illustration of the August 6, 1898, *Judge* magazine, portraying U.S. supremacy in the Philippines as a butterfly emerging from Dewey's victory in Manila Bay

HE CAN'T CATCH IT

Below: Roosevelt (right) during the Spanish-American War. With him are (left to right) Major Brodie, Major Dunn, Major General Wheeler, and an unidentified clergyman.

During the next two days the U.S. Cavalry Division marched through the inland Cuban jungle. Suddenly on June 24, along a road called Camino Real, the Spanish enemy attacked. Traveling with the Rough Riders, reporter Richard Harding Davis exclaimed, "we were caught in a clear case of ambush . . . the hottest, nastiest fight I ever imagined." Snipers shot down several Rough Riders around Roosevelt. As soon as the lieutenant colonel located the entrenched enemy position he ordered his troops to charge. "We advanced firing at them," declared Roosevelt, "and drove them off." In this skirmish, called the Battle of Las Guasimas, sixteen Rough Riders fell dead and fifty more lay wounded. Still Roosevelt boasted, "we wanted first whack at the Spaniards and we got it." During the next few days the Americans regrouped and plotted strategy.

July 1, 1898, dawned hot and muggy. As the army started its final push toward Santiago, distant Spanish cannon rained fragmenting shells upon the troops. Jagged shrapnel flying through the air killed and wounded a number of Rough Riders. "One of the shrapnel bullets," remarked Roosevelt, "fell on my wrist and raised a bump as big as a hickory nut."

Tramping forward through the jungle the Rough Riders reached muddy San Juan Creek. Beyond rose the heavily defended San Juan Heights. Roosevelt waited impatiently as gunfire cut up his ranks. Receiving his orders at last, the brave Rough Rider recklessly led the charge that conquered Kettle Hill. Not content, he next hurried his men and other troops ahead to join the storming of San Juan

Roosevelt and his Rough Riders at San Juan Hill

Hill. "I killed a Spaniard with my own hand like a jackrabbit," he exclaimed afterwards. "It was a miracle of self-sacrifice," declared Richard Harding Davis of the fiery battle, "a triumph of bulldog courage." Completely stunned, the Spaniards at last fled the hills for the safety of Santiago. "Look at those . . . Spanish dead," pointed out Roosevelt as he victoriously examined the bloody, abandoned trenches. Years later he could honestly declare, "San Juan was the great day of my life."

Thanks to the American army's success—and to the U.S. Navy's destruction of the Spanish fleet in Santiago harbor soon after—the war in Cuba ended just two weeks later. Promoted to full colonel, Roosevelt soon wrote an urgent letter to the War Department describing the danger of yellow fever if the army remained encamped in Cuba. Within days the troops boarded ships for home.

On August 15, 1898, the American troops disembarked at Montauk, Long Island. "Roosevelt! Roosevelt! Hurrah for Teddy and the Rough Riders!" excitedly shouted the waiting crowd. The heroic charge up San Juan Hill had made Roosevelt an instant national hero, the greatest to come out of the war. Within days, New York Republicans approached the colonel and asked him to accept the nomination for governor. Mustered out of the army and thinking of his future, Roosevelt promptly agreed.

With boundless energy Roosevelt plunged into the fall campaign. By train he stumped back and forth across the state. To help draw crowds, seven uniformed Rough Riders, including a bugler, traveled with him. "You have heard the trumpet that sounded to bring you here," he exhorted voters in one town. "I have heard it tear the tropic dawn when it summoned us to fight at Santiago."

Making a dozen speeches a day, shaking hundreds of hands, and roaring by train through town after town, Roosevelt worked right up to election day. When the ballots were counted, it was found he had overcome his Democratic opponent by 17,794 votes. "I am more than contented to be Governor of New York," he announced, "and shall not care if I never hold another office."

Theodore Roosevelt at his desk

At the age of forty, Roosevelt returned to Albany and took up his new duties. Throughout the year of 1899, he urged state laws to cut the long working hours of women and children, clean up city sweatshops, and promote the merit system in the civil service. Old-guard Republicans ranted when the young governor signed legislation to tax corporations in the state. Pleased with his triumphs over these politicians, Roosevelt commented, "I have always been fond of the West African proverb: 'Speak softly and carry a big stick, you will go far.' "

President McKinley discusses campaign plans with running mate Roosevelt.

New York senator Thomas Platt, the state's Republican party boss, decided Roosevelt was going *too* far. "I don't want him raising hell in my state any longer," he complained. When Vice-President Garret Hobart suddenly died in November 1899, Senator Platt saw a chance to push the troublemaking governor out of state politics. He urged Roosevelt to run for vice-president on William McKinley's 1900 election ticket. "Under no circumstances," responded Roosevelt, "could I or would I accept the nomination for the Vice-Presidency." To a friend he confided, "The Vice-Presidency is not an office in which I could *do* anything. . . ."

Arriving as a delegate at the June 1900 Republican National Convention in Philadelphia, Roosevelt discovered that Republicans nationwide wanted him as the vice-presidential candidate. Cheers for the Rough Rider thrilled him. Senator Platt happily observed, "Roosevelt might as well stand under Niagara Falls and try to spit water back as to stop his nomination by this convention." The Republican national chairman, Ohio senator Mark Hanna, however, feared Roosevelt's reputation for wildness.

"Don't any of you realize," he thundered, "there's only one life between this madman and the White House?"

In the end, by a vote of 925 to 1, the convention nominated Roosevelt to run with President McKinley. Roosevelt alone refused to vote for himself. Although he imagined he would become a forgotten man as vice-president, still Roosevelt charged enthusiastically into the 1900 election campaign. While McKinley attacked his Democratic opponent, William Jennings Bryan, in a few speeches delivered from his Canton, Ohio, front porch, Roosevelt stampeded across the country. Traveling over 21,000 miles, he thrilled the public with 673 speeches in 567 towns in 24 states before November 3. "'Tis Teddy alone that's runnin'," exclaimed American humorist Finley Peter Dunne, "and he ain't r'runnin', he's gallopin'."

McKinley easily won reelection as president. On March 4, 1901, Roosevelt took the oath of office as vice-president of the United States in Washington, D.C. For five brief days he presided over a special session of the Senate. Then when the Senate adjourned, he returned to New York to vacation with friends and family. Completely bored, Roosevelt complained that the vice-presidency was an office that "ought to be abolished."

Before the summer ended, however, a national tragedy changed the vice-president's life completely. On September 6 President McKinley visited the grand Pan-American Exposition in Buffalo, New York. As he greeted people on a reception line, a crazed anarchist named Leon Czolgosz stepped up and shot him twice with a pistol. Upon learning this horrible news, Roosevelt hurried to Buffalo.

Doctors attending McKinley discovered that the first bullet only had grazed his ribs, while the second had torn deeply through his stomach. Though he was gravely injured, the president slowly seemed to improve. To ease the minds of worried Americans, Roosevelt left Buffalo on September 10 to go camping with his family.

In New York's remote Adirondack Mountains, Roosevelt lodged at Camp Tahawus. On Friday, September 13, he completed a rugged hike up 5,344-foot Mount Marcy, the highest peak in the state. While lunching beside a mountain lake Roosevelt spied a ranger hurrying up the trail with a telegram. "THE PRESIDENT'S CONDITION HAS CHANGED FOR THE WORSE," read the message.

"I must go back at once," announced the vice-president.

Through the night Roosevelt rushed by horse-drawn buckboard along twisting mountain roads. Although the open carriage easily could have hurtled over a cliff in the dark, he urged his drivers, "If you are not afraid, I'm not. Push ahead!" At breakneck speed, the buckboard raced forty miles by morning. When he arrived at the nearest railroad station, the worst possible news greeted him. To his wife he promptly wired, "PRESIDENT MCKINLEY DIED AT 2:15 THIS MORNING."

A gun in his bandaged right hand, Leon Czolgosz shoots President McKinley point-blank on September 9, 1901. Czolgosz was executed on October 29, 1901.

On a special train Roosevelt steamed ahead to Buffalo. That evening, September 14, 1901, in the Buffalo home of Ansley Wilcox, Roosevelt took the oath of office as twenty-sixth president. At the age of forty-two, he had become the youngest president in United States history. To grieving cabinet members Roosevelt solemnly stated, "I wish to say that it shall be my aim to continue, absolutely unbroken, the policy of President McKinley for the peace, the prosperity, and the honor of our country."

Unconvinced, Senator Mark Hanna recalled his convention warning. "Now look," he angrily cried, "that damned cowboy is President of the United States!"

Left: Edith Roosevelt, Theodore's second wife

Below: The Roosevelt family at Sagamore Hill in 1903—left to right are Quentin, age 5; Theodore, 44; Theodore, Jr., 15; Archie, 9; Alice, 19; Kermit, 13; Edith, 41; and Ethel, 11.

Opposite page: Theodore holds his grandson Archibald Roosevelt, Jr., as the baby's mother looks over his shoulder. Next to her is Edith Roosevelt. On the right is Theodore's daughter Ethel Roosevelt Derby. Her two children, sitting on laps, are Richard Derby, Jr., and Edith Derby.

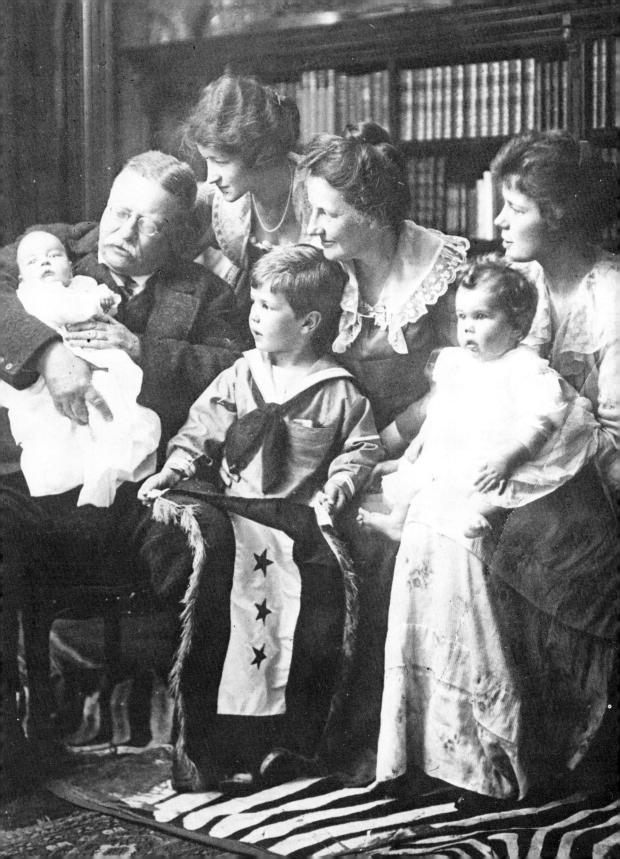

Chapter 6

Wielding a Big Stick

"It is a dreadful thing to come into the Presidency this way," remarked Roosevelt, "but it would be a far worse thing to be morbid about it. Here is the task, and I have got to do it to the best of my ability; and that is all there is about it."

Popularly referred to as "TR" by the press and as "Teddy" by the public, President Roosevelt immediately captured the attention of Americans. For years the President's Mansion (soon to be known officially as the White House) had been occupied by dignified, older men. Now Roosevelt surprised everyone with his bursting physical activity.

For indoor exercise Roosevelt still enjoyed pulling on a pair of boxing gloves. For two hours every morning he traded punches with sparring partners. One day, though, he received a bad blow that caused gradual blindness in his left eye. After that he stopped boxing, only to study jujitsu wrestling instead. Sometimes friends practiced with him. On one occasion the president watched with amusement as a small Japanese jujitsu instructor expertly spun giant, three-hundred-pound Secretary of War William Howard Taft to the floor.

President Roosevelt and his horse, 1902

Out of doors Roosevelt loved to take long hikes. Insisting on following a straight line, climbing over or under everything in the way, he called these travels "obstacle walks." Well-dressed diplomats invited to stroll with the president often found themselves scrambling through rocky woods. "My arms and shoulders are still stiff with dragging myself up by roots and ledges," recalled British ambassador Sir Mortimer Durand of one such ramble.

French ambassador Jean-Jules Jusserand long remembered another day's exercise. After playing two sets of tennis, Roosevelt suggested they jog on the White House lawn. Next they tossed a heavy medicine ball back and forth, and then the president asked, "What would you like to do now?" "If it's just the same with you, Mr. President," groaned Jusserand, "I'd like to lie down and die."

Americans found such energy quite refreshing in their president. "He was pure act," described writer Henry Adams. Happy and robust, Roosevelt urged all Americans to join him in what he called "The Strenuous Life."

One of Roosevelt's first acts as president was to invite black educator Booker T. Washington to have dinner at the White House on October 16, 1901. No black man had ever done that before, and white southerners—still angry thirty-six years after the American Civil War had ended slavery—raged about the incident. In answer, Roosevelt privately blustered that he would have Dr. Washington "to dine just as often as I please."

The president's progressive spirit also upset America's most powerful business leaders. In his first message to Congress Roosevelt stated, "There is a widespread conviction in the minds of the American people that the great corporations known as trusts are in certain of their features and tendencies hurtful to the general welfare." Acting under the Sherman Antitrust Act of 1890, Roosevelt soon filed suit against the Northern Securities Company. Controlled by financier J. P. Morgan, this trust hoped to monopolize the railroads of the Northwest, forcing higher transportation prices.

When he learned of the suit, Morgan hurried to the White House. "We can easily compromise the matter," he smoothly assured the president. Bluntly Roosevelt responded, "There can be no compromise in the enforcement of the law." In 1904 the Supreme Court ruled that the Northern Securities Company must be dissolved.

In the beef, oil, and tobacco industries, Roosevelt attacked other illegal monopolies, which the courts broke up or heavily fined. In 1903 he formed the Department of Commerce and Labor to help protect the rights of consumers and laborers. When Oscar Straus was named its secretary in 1906, he became the first Jewish person to hold a U.S. cabinet position.

Roosevelt wielded his "big stick" in other areas as well. In May 1902, work in Pennsylvania's anthracite coal mines suddenly halted as 140,000 members of the United Mine Workers Union formed picket lines to strike. After enduring years of unsafe work conditions at low wages, these men demanded better treatment. As stockpiles of coal disappeared and cold weather approached, Roosevelt predicted "the most terrible riots that this country has ever seen."

Though he had no legal right to interfere in the strike, in October Roosevelt called union leaders and mine representatives to Washington to talk. Mine operator George Baer stiffly refused to give in to any of the strikers' demands. "If it wasn't for the high office I hold," angrily commented Roosevelt, "I would have taken him by the seat of the breeches and the nape of the neck and chucked him out of that window."

A 1906 cartoon showing Roosevelt's attitude toward monopolies

Finally, to prevent national disaster, Roosevelt threatened to use the National Guard to work the mines. At last the mine owners agreed to let a panel of arbitrators decide the issue. The panel announced a 10-percent increase in workers' wages, and the miners returned to work. Of his vigorous role in the crisis Roosevelt stated, "My business is to see fair play among all men, capitalists or wageworkers." All he wanted, he claimed, was "to see to it that every man has a square deal, no more and no less." Admiring Americans roundly applauded Roosevelt's "Square Deal" policies.

As the United States entered the 1900s, great advances occurred in the field of transportation. Newfangled horse-less carriages called "automobiles" rattled over roads, while across the sand dunes at Kitty Hawk, North Carolina, Orville and Wilbur Wright successfully launched a motorized airplane on December 17, 1903, proving that humans could fly. To speed world travel and bolster commerce, Roosevelt urged the building of a canal across Central America to connect the Atlantic and the Pacific oceans. Engineers decided that the best place to dig would be across Panama, at that time part of Colombia. With the approval of Congress, Roosevelt opened negotia-tions with the Colombian government. Colombian leaders, however, kept demanding more and more money for the rights to a ten-mile-wide Canal Zone. Later Roosevelt impatiently exclaimed, "You could no more make an agreement with the Colombian rulers than you could nail currant jelly to a wall."

Finally, with Roosevelt's quiet encouragement, Panama-nian revolutionaries took to the streets on November 3, 1903. When they declared their independence from Co-lombia, U.S. warships protected the new republic of Panama. Soon the grateful Panamanian government agreed to a treaty, and construction began in the U.S. Canal Zone. Later Roosevelt proudly remarked, "I took Panama without consulting the Cabinet." He defended his actions by stating, "If I had followed traditional, conserva-tive methods . . . the debate would have been going on yet. But I took the Canal Zone, and let Congress debate, and while the debate goes on the canal does also."

Above: The Wright brothers, Orville (on plane) and Wilbur (right), fly the *Kitty Hawk* on December 17, 1903. Below: The Panama Canal opens on August 15, 1914.

Chapter 7

Adventurous Presidency

"President of the United States!" declared Roosevelt in his forceful, clear-cut style of speech. "I'd rather be *e-lected* to that office than have anything tangible of which I know." As the 1904 election season approached, personal friend Henry Adams noted, "Theodore has stopped talking cowboy and San Juan. Every idea centers now on the election, and he talks about that with all the fluency . . . of a schoolboy." His enormous popularity swelling, when the Republican national convention convened in Chicago in June 1904, the delegates unanimously nominated Roosevelt to run for a full term as president. For vice-president they chose Indiana senator Charles W. Fairbanks.

To oppose Roosevelt, the Democrats picked New York judge Alton B. Parker to run for president. "I think Parker will be as handy for us to beat as anyone," remarked Massachusetts senator Henry Cabot Lodge to Roosevelt. While dignity required that Roosevelt remain at the White House, Judge Parker conducted a dull campaign and never had a chance.

On November 8, 1904, Americans called the Rough Rider back to office by an overwhelming vote. When the ballots were tallied they revealed the following counts:

	Popular Vote	Electoral Vote
Theodore Roosevelt	7,623,486	336
Alton B. Parker	5,077,911	140

On the eve of his inauguration Roosevelt gleefully exclaimed, "Tomorrow I shall come into my office in my own right. Then watch out for me!"

The crisp, cold weather of March 4, 1905, did not stop hundreds of thousands of people from gathering in Washington for Roosevelt's inauguration. On the east portico of the Capitol, Supreme Court Chief Justice Melville Fuller administered the oath of office. Then Roosevelt stepped forward to deliver his inaugural address. As Americans, Roosevelt proclaimed, "we have duties to others and duties to ourselves; and we shirk neither. . . . Toward all other nations, large and small, our attitude must be one of cordial and sincere friendship. . . . But justice and generosity in a nation . . . count most when shown not by the weak but by the strong."

In the parade that followed, Rough Rider veterans thrilled Roosevelt by galloping past the reviewing stand. Some stopped and leaned from their saddles to shake hands with their beloved colonel. Caught up in the excitement, Americans braced themselves for four more years of Theodore Roosevelt.

Nothing the president did escaped the notice of the public. During a hunting trip in Mississippi, Roosevelt refused

Nicholas Longworth, Alice Roosevelt, and the proud father.

to shoot a helpless bear cub. Soon stores all across the country were selling toy "Teddy bears." White House staff member Archie Butt exclaimed, "We woke up every morning wondering what new adventure we were off on when Roosevelt was President."

Roosevelt's lively family accounted for a good part of the fun. Alice Roosevelt had grown into an independent and beautiful young woman. Of her high spirits Roosevelt joked, "I can do one of two things, I can be President of the United States, or I can control Alice. I cannot possibly do both." Adored by the public, the press dubbed her "Princess Alice." Her White House wedding in 1906 to Congressman Nicholas Longworth was a national event.

Roosevelt's younger children, Theodore, Jr., Kermit, Ethel, Archie, and Quentin, became known as "The White House Gang." Together they raced on the stairs, slid down the banisters, roller-skated in the hallways, and walked about the mansion on stilts. The children kept a wide variety of pets, including dogs, cats, snakes, a guinea pig, and a kangaroo rat. Once when Archie lay sick in bed, the family pony, Algonquin, was smuggled upstairs in the elevator to visit him.

It was Mrs. Roosevelt who brought a sense of grace and elegance to the White House. As First Lady she supervised an extensive remodeling of the mansion. She managed the household budget and weekly musical entertainments and spent, as Archie Butt remembered, "seven years in the White House without making a mistake."

By 1904 the United States had taken its place among the world's great powers, and Roosevelt remained keenly interested in foreign affairs. Already he had settled a boundary dispute between the Alaska Territory and Canada. Later he assured democracy in free Cuba by sending peacekeeping troops there. In 1905, however, he performed his greatest service as a peacemaker.

For over a year Russian and Japanese troops had been locked in a bloody war for control of Manchuria and Korea. To bring calm to the Pacific region, Roosevelt prevailed upon the two nations to enter into peace negotiations. In the summer of 1905 Roosevelt hosted Japanese and Russian diplomats as they met in Portsmouth, New Hampshire. "Dealing with senators," confided the president, "is at times excellent training for the temper, but

Fifty years of U.S.-Japanese relations: Officials meet to open trade relations in 1854 (above); Roosevelt helps resolve the Russo-Japanese War (below).

upon my word dealing with these peace envoys has been an even tougher job." After many difficult days the two nations agreed on peace. For his important part in ending the Russo-Japanese War, Roosevelt won the 1906 Nobel Peace Prize.

American relations with Japan grew tense in 1907. The children of thousands of poor Japanese immigrants were filling California schools to overflowing. In an informal "gentleman's agreement," Roosevelt persuaded Japan to reduce the number of laborers leaving its shores every year. To help calm the situation, Roosevelt dispatched a huge U.S. fleet of sixteen battleships on a worldwide "courtesy" cruise, including a friendly stop in Japan.

Across the United States in the early 1900s, crusading journalists like Lincoln Steffens and Ida Tarbell were exposing the evils of American politics and business. Roosevelt labeled these writers "muckrakers," because they raked up filth for the public to view. One book in particular, *The Jungle* by Upton Sinclair, aroused public disgust when it revealed the ugly, unhealthy conditions in America's meatpacking companies.

As a result of the muckrakers' exposures, in 1906 Roosevelt forced passage of the Pure Food and Drug Act, which outlawed the manufacture and sale of impure food, drugs, or medicines. He also passed a new Meat Inspection Act, which gave health inspectors the right to examine stockyards and meatpacking houses. Another law was the Hepburn Act of 1906. This bill strengthened the ability of the Interstate Commerce Commission to control unsafe and unfair railroad practices.

President Roosevelt (left) on his tour of the West

"Is there any law that will prevent me from declaring Pelican Island a Federal Bird Reservation?" questioned Roosevelt one day. "Very well, then I so declare it!" As president, Roosevelt made great strides to protect America's wildlife. In 1903, Pelican Island in Florida became the first of fifty game preserves he established.

After a visit out West Roosevelt exclaimed, "There is nothing in the world more beautiful than Yosemite . . . groves of giant Sequoias and redwoods . . . the people should see to it that they are preserved for their children and their children's children." Roosevelt designated that valley a national park in 1906. That same year he made Devils Tower in Wyoming America's first national monument. In all, he reserved 150,000,000 acres of land for national use. Doubling the number of national parks, he earned the nickname "the Great Conservationist."

Roosevelt (center) visits the Panama Canal construction site.

As Roosevelt neared the end of his term he could look
back over his many accomplishments with pride. In 1907
Oklahoma joined the United States, adding the forty-sixth
star to the American flag. A year earlier Roosevelt traveled
south to inspect progress on the Panama Canal. The visit
made him the first president to leave the United States
while in office. In the Panama jungle 43,000 workers
labored on the fifty-mile canal project, which would not be
finished until 1914. To his son he wrote, "They are eating
steadily into the mountain, cutting it down and down."

Roosevelt addressing sailors who have just arrived from their goodwill cruise

In February 1909 Roosevelt hailed the return of the "Great White Fleet" from its peaceful around-the-world cruise. These powerful battleships cutting through the ocean waves openly proclaimed that America was "the mightiest republic on which the sun ever shone." As he watched the fleet's arrival at Hampton Roads, Virginia, Roosevelt joyfully roared, "Here they are. . . . I could not ask a finer concluding scene to my administration."

Chapter 8

Bull Moose Candidate

"No President has ever enjoyed himself as much as I have enjoyed myself," declared Roosevelt, "and for the matter of that I do not know any man of my age who has had as good a time."

Throughout his term of office, Roosevelt insisted he would not accept another nomination in 1908. The hugely popular and powerful president, however, did want to see his political programs continued. Therefore, he hand-picked his close friend Secretary of War William Howard Taft to follow in his footsteps. With Roosevelt's open support, Taft easily won the 1908 Republican presidential nomination on the first ballot. From the White House, Roosevelt recommended Taft to the people. "He is not only absolutely fearless, absolutely disinterested and upright, but he has the widest acquaintance with the nation's needs." In the general election in November 1908, Taft easily beat William Jennings Bryan, whom the Democrats had picked to run for the third time.

Opposite page: Roosevelt and rhino in Sotik, Africa, 1909

Kermit and Theodore pose with Roosevelt's first buffalo, whose head is still on the library wall at Sagamore Hill, now a national historic site.

A year before leaving the presidency, Roosevelt began planning a long African safari. This trip, he believed, would be his "last chance for something in the nature of a 'great adventure.' " The Smithsonian Institution agreed to sponsor the expedition, and on March 23, 1909, only three weeks after quitting the White House, Roosevelt and his nineteen-year-old son, Kermit, excitedly sailed off to start their big game hunt.

Accompanied by taxidermists, naturalists, guides, and two hundred native porters, the Roosevelts crossed the vast plains of present-day Kenya and afterwards chopped their way through the steaming jungle to the north, eventually reaching the Nile River. Shooting his first lion gave

Roosevelt particular pleasure. "Down he came," exclaimed the thrilled hunter, "sixty yards off, his hind quarters dragging, his head up, his ears back, his jaws open and lips drawn up in a . . . snarl."

For ten months the father and son hunted "the mighty and terrible lords of the wilderness." Together they killed over five hundred animals and birds, including elephants, hippos, and seventeen lions. Roosevelt delightedly wrote home that he had discovered a valuable occupation for ex-presidents. "They can be used to scare rhinos away." Along with hundreds of plant specimens, Roosevelt preserved most of his African trophies for Smithsonian museum exhibits.

Emerging at last from Africa, Roosevelt next conducted a grand tour of Europe. In Germany he reviewed army maneuvers with Kaiser Wilhelm. In Sweden he formally accepted his Nobel Peace Prize. In England he attended the funeral of King Edward VII. Everywhere he visited, Europe's royalty warmly greeted him. Amused, yet wearied, by all of the pomp and ceremony, he later commented, "I felt that if I met another king I should bite him."

Huge American crowds gathered in New York City to welcome Roosevelt back from his foreign journeys in June 1910. In a spectacular parade along Fifth Avenue, they cheered the return of "the colonel," as he was now commonly called.

Finally reaching Sagamore Hill, the famous world traveler claimed, "All I want now is privacy. I want to close up like a native oyster."

The first president to fly in an airplane, Roosevelt took a thrill-packed three-minute ride.

National politics, though, continued to hold his attention. During a cross-country speaking tour in the summer and fall of 1910, he called for radical government reforms. While visiting Lambert Field near Saint Louis on October 11, Roosevelt soared up into the sky in an airplane, the first president ever to fly. "It was great! First class!" he afterwards exclaimed, pumping the pilot's hand.

In time Roosevelt grew displeased with the way President Taft was running the government. Government workers and policies from the Roosevelt years were being cast aside. As the 1912 election approached, Roosevelt announced his willingness to run again. To one reporter he enthusiastically stated, "My hat is in the ring."

In this 1912 cartoon, Roosevelt
and Taft fight for the presidency.
Uncle Sam, looking on, says,
"I guess old friends are the best!"

Many wealthy and powerful Republicans worried about
Roosevelt's radical ideas. Amassing delegate strength, at
the national Republican convention in Chicago these men
assured Taft's renomination on the first ballot. Roosevelt
supporters cried out that the nomination had been stolen.
In answer the colonel promised, "If you wish me to make
the fight I will." Gladly Roosevelt accepted the nomination
from the newly-formed Progressive party. After he
exclaimed to reporters that he felt as strong as a bull
moose, this party became known as the Bull Moose party.

Campaigning in 1912

"Win or lose we shall not falter," insisted the Bull Moose candidate. Included in his political platform were demands for direct elections, an inheritance tax, more powerful labor unions, and the right of women to vote. The Democratic party nominated popular New Jersey governor Woodrow Wilson for president. Wilson's liberal political platform also appealed to the masses. With Roosevelt and Taft splitting the Republican vote, Wilson seemed certain to win the election.

In spite of that, fifty-three-year-old Roosevelt stormed across the nation giving one fiery speech after another. On October 14, 1912, the campaign trail took him to Milwaukee, Wisconsin. As Roosevelt climbed into an open car in front of the Hotel Gilpatrick, an assassin standing in the nearby crowd leaned forward and fired a pistol. The bullet struck Roosevelt in the chest. As bystanders knocked the gunman, John F. Schrank, to the ground, he yelled that no man should be allowed a third term as president.

Immediately people rushed to Roosevelt's side. Still standing in the car, he examined himself. The bullet had ripped through the pages of the prepared speech in his breast pocket. Then it had torn through a metal spectacle case. Slowed by these items, the bullet next broke a rib before stopping near his right lung. Stubbornly Roosevelt insisted on continuing to the city auditorium. "I have a message to deliver and I will deliver it as long as there is life in my body," he rasped. Before a shocked and worried audience Roosevelt gave his speech. Only afterwards would the bleeding man agree to go to the hospital.

Recovery from the wound halted Roosevelt's campaigning. Most people realized anyway that he had little chance of winning. On election day, November 5, 1912, Americans chose their next president, and soon banner newspaper headlines reported the results:

	Popular Vote	Electoral Vote
Woodrow Wilson	6,293,454	435
Theodore Roosevelt	4,119,538	88
William Howard Taft	3,484,980	8

Although Roosevelt had beaten Taft, Wilson and the Democrats had proven triumphant over both. Roosevelt's daughter, Alice, sadly remarked of the idealistic Bull Moose campaign, "We had the conviction and vision, but alas, not the votes."

Chapter 9

The Lion Is Dead

In retirement Roosevelt kept as active as ever. In 1913 he wrote his autobiography and tramped through the Grand Canyon on a camping trip with his youngest sons. Then toward the end of the year he grabbed at a "last chance to be a boy." A party of explorers, headed by Colonel Candido Rincon, intended to investigate uncharted areas of the Brazilian jungle. Roosevelt and his son Kermit gladly joined this South American expedition.

On January 15, 1914, the explorers reached the farthest outpost on the Paraguay River. For a month they slowly pushed ahead through the jungle until at last they reached the River of Doubt. Collecting dugout canoes and food supplies, they prepared to travel on the river and discover where it led. "We were about to go into the unknown," marveled Roosevelt, "and no one could say what it held."

The journey would prove both hard and dangerous. Through the next days the canoes cruised on the current through "a lofty and matted forest [that] rose like a green wall on either hand." Often the party encountered rapids and waterfalls. One rough stretch of water overturned Kermit's canoe, causing a Brazilian porter to drown.

Along the tangled jungle route, native Indians lurked with poisoned arrows. Exhaustion, heat, and hunger frayed the nerves of party members. On April 5 Roosevelt suffered a serious accident. To save a dugout from hitting rocks, Roosevelt jumped into the water. A sharp stone gashed his leg. The injury swelled, and gradually Roosevelt developed a fever. Through the next days the men trudged on, as Roosevelt's condition worsened. Finally the colonel told his son, "I want you . . . to go ahead. We have reached a point where some of us must stop. I feel I am only a burden to the party."

Of course Kermit refused to leave his father behind to die. In the middle of April, after traveling 1,500 miles, the struggling explorers at last reached the Amazon River and civilization. The men carried Roosevelt out of the jungle on a stretcher and slowly his health improved. For his success in tracing the course of the River of Doubt, the Brazilian government honored the ex-president by renaming the river Rio Roosevelt.

Back at Sagamore Hill the colonel regained his strength and energy. Continuing a lifelong habit, he read a new book almost every day. At his desk he wrote of his Brazilian adventures and edited magazine articles on political affairs. On many delightful evenings he entertained friends and guests at the dinner table or in the trophy room of the house, which was adorned with buffalo heads and leopard skins.

In August 1914, world war erupted among the nations of Europe. Immediately Roosevelt warned Americans to prepare to join the war as an ally of Britain and France

Roosevelt addressing 29,000 soldiers during World War I before they go off to France

against Germany. The old Rough Rider's feelings grew even more fierce when a German submarine torpedoed the British oceanliner *Lusitania* without warning on May 7, 1915. Among the 1,200 passengers killed during the sinking were 128 Americans. Roosevelt called the tragedy "murder on the high seas." In the spring of 1917, German submarines began attacking American ships as well. At President Wilson's urging, Congress at last declared war against Germany on April 6, 1917.

His warrior's blood aroused, Roosevelt sought a commission as a major general. To the secretary of war he wrote, "I . . . earnestly ask permission to raise a division for immediate service at the front." President Wilson, Roosevelt's longtime political enemy, strongly resisted the idea. "Colonel Roosevelt is a splendid man and a patriotic citizen," conceded Wilson, "but he is not a military leader." His request to raise a division denied, Roosevelt bitterly claimed, "I am the only one he has kept out of war."

Within the Roosevelt family this was certainly true. All four of the colonel's sons received army commissions. At a patriotic rally in New York Roosevelt responded to a heckler by saying, "What am I doing for my country in the war? I have sent my four boys over there. I have sent my four boys, for each of whose lives I care a thousand times more than I care for my own." As his sons fought in Europe, a friend teased him, "The first thing you know, your four sons will put the name Roosevelt on the map."

On July 17, 1918, however, came tragic news. Twenty-year-old Quentin Roosevelt, an air force pilot, had been shot down over France and killed. The loss of his youngest son overwhelmed Roosevelt with sadness. "There is no use of my writing about Quentin," he grieved, "for I should break down if I tried."

Gradually Roosevelt's spirit and health did break down. On November 11, 1918, the day World War I ended with Allied victory, he entered the hospital complaining of aching joints. This rheumatism, along with a middle-ear infection that left him partially deaf, and continued soreness in his old leg injury, greatly weakened him.

Roosevelt in a rowboat at Oyster Bay

Returning to Sagamore Hill Roosevelt told his sister Corinne, "Well, anyway, no matter what comes, I have kept the promise I made to myself when I was twenty-one . . . that I would work *up to the hilt* until I was sixty, and I have done it." On the evening of January 5, 1919, he dictated a newspaper editorial and then retired. Lying comfortably at last, he asked his valet, James Amos, "Please put out the light." At four o'clock in the morning, January 6, 1919, sixty-year-old Theodore Roosevelt died when a blood clot clogged an artery leading to his heart.

"THE LION IS DEAD," cabled Archie Roosevelt to his brothers still in France. Newspapers quickly spread the sad news and flags across the country fluttered to half mast. "Death had to take him sleeping," remarked Vice-President Thomas R. Marshall, "for if Roosevelt had been awake, there would have been a fight."

Roosevelt's grave in the Oyster Bay Cemetery on Long Island

All the nation mourned as friends and family saw Roosevelt buried at Young's Memorial Cemetery in Oyster Bay. In a tribute that spoke the feelings of millions, journalist William Allen White wrote, "I have never known such a man as he. . . . He poured into my heart such visions, such ideals, such hopes, such a new attitude toward life and patriotism . . . as I had never dreamed men had."

The progressive politics of Theodore Roosevelt had helped thrust the United States into the modern age. Perhaps his greatest gift to Americans, however, is the memory of his honest vigor and constant joy of life.

Chronology of American History

(Shaded area covers events in Theodore Roosevelt's lifetime.)

About A.D. 982—Eric the Red, born in Norway, reaches Greenland in one of the first European voyages to North America.

About 985—Eric the Red brings settlers from Iceland to Greenland.

About 1000—Leif Ericson (Eric the Red's son) leads what is thought to be the first European expedition to mainland North America; Leif probably lands in Canada.

1492—Christopher Columbus, seeking a sea route from Spain to the Far East, discovers the New World.

1497—John Cabot reaches Canada in the first English voyage to North America.

1513—Ponce de Léon explores Florida in search of the fabled Fountain of Youth.

1519-1521—Hernando Cortés of Spain conquers Mexico.

1534—French explorers led by Jacques Cartier enter the Gulf of St. Lawrence in Canada.

1540—Spanish explorer Francisco Coronado begins exploring the American Southwest, seeking the riches of the mythical Seven Cities of Cibola.

1565—St. Augustine, Florida, the first permanent European town in what is now the United States, is founded by the Spanish.

1607—Jamestown, Virginia, is founded, the first permanent English town in the present-day U.S.

1608—Frenchman Samuel de Champlain founds the village of Quebec, Canada.

1609—Henry Hudson explores the eastern coast of present-day U.S. for the Netherlands; the Dutch then claim parts of New York, New Jersey, Delaware, and Connecticut and name the area New Netherland.

1619—The English colonies' first shipment of black slaves arrives in Jamestown.

1620—English Pilgrims found Massachusetts' first permanent town at Plymouth.

1621—Massachusetts Pilgrims and Indians hold the famous first Thanksgiving feast in colonial America.

1623—Colonization of New Hampshire is begun by the English.

1624—Colonization of present-day New York State is begun by the Dutch at Fort Orange (Albany).

1625—The Dutch start building New Amsterdam (now New York City).

1630—The town of Boston, Massachusetts, is founded by the English Puritans.

1633—Colonization of Connecticut is begun by the English.

1634—Colonization of Maryland is begun by the English.

1636—Harvard, the colonies' first college, is founded in Massachusetts. Rhode Island colonization begins when Englishman Roger Williams founds Providence.

1638—Delaware colonization begins when Swedish people build Fort Christina at present-day Wilmington.

1640—Stephen Daye of Cambridge, Massachusetts prints *The Bay Psalm Book*, the first English-language book published in what is now the U.S.

1643—Swedish settlers begin colonizing Pennsylvania.

About 1650—North Carolina is colonized by Virginia settlers.

1660—New Jersey colonization is begun by the Dutch at present-day Jersey City.

1670—South Carolina colonization is begun by the English near Charleston.

1673—Jacques Marquette and Louis Jolliet explore the upper Mississippi River for France.

1682—Philadelphia, Pennsylvania, is settled. La Salle explores Mississippi River all the way to its mouth in Louisiana and claims the whole Mississippi Valley for France.

1693—College of William and Mary is founded in Williamsburg, Virginia.

1700—Colonial population is about 250,000.

1703—Benjamin Franklin is born in Boston.

1732—George Washington, first president of the U.S., is born in Westmoreland County, Virginia.

1733—James Oglethorpe founds Savannah, Georgia; Georgia is established as the thirteenth colony.

1735—John Adams, second president of the U.S., is born in Braintree, Massachusetts.

1737—William Byrd founds Richmond, Virginia.

1738—British troops are sent to Georgia over border dispute with Spain.

1739—Black insurrection takes place in South Carolina.

1740—English Parliament passes act allowing naturalization of immigrants to American colonies after seven-year residence.

1743—Thomas Jefferson, third president of the U.S., is born in Albemarle County, Virginia. Benjamin Franklin retires at age thirty-seven to devote himself to scientific inquiries and public service.

1744—King George's War begins; France joins war effort against England.

1745—During King George's War, France raids settlements in Maine and New York.

1747—Classes begin at Princeton College in New Jersey.

1748—The Treaty of Aix-la-Chapelle concludes King George's War.

1749—Parliament legally recognizes slavery in colonies and the inauguration of the plantation system in the South. George Washington becomes the surveyor for Culpepper County in Virginia.

1750—Thomas Walker passes through and names Cumberland Gap on his way toward Kentucky region. Colonial population is about 1,200,000.

1751—James Madison, fourth president of the U.S., is born in Port Conway, Virginia. English Parliament passes Currency Act, banning New England colonies from issuing paper money. George Washington travels to Barbados.

1752—Pennsylvania Hospital, the first general hospital in the colonies, is founded in Philadelphia. Benjamin Franklin uses a kite in a thunderstorm to demonstrate that lightning is a form of electricity.

1753—George Washington delivers command from Virginia Lieutenant Governor Dinwiddie that the French withdraw from the Ohio River Valley; French disregard the demand. Colonial population is about 1,328,000.

1754—French and Indian War begins (extends to Europe as the Seven Years' War). Washington surrenders at Fort Necessity.

1755—French and Indians ambush General Braddock. Washington becomes commander of Virginia troops.

1756—England declares war on France.

1758—James Monroe, fifth president of the U.S., is born in Westmoreland County, Virginia.

1759—Cherokee Indian war begins in southern colonies; hostilities extend to 1761. George Washington marries Martha Dandridge Custis.

1760—George III becomes king of England. Colonial population is about 1,600,000.

1762—England declares war on Spain.

1763—Treaty of Paris concludes the French and Indian War and the Seven Years' War. England gains Canada and most other French lands east of the Mississippi River.

1764—British pass the Sugar Act to gain tax money from the colonists. The issue of taxation without representation is first introduced in Boston. John Adams marries Abigail Smith.

1765—Stamp Act goes into effect in the colonies. Business virtually stops as almost all colonists refuse to use the stamps.

1766—British repeal the Stamp Act.

1767—John Quincy Adams, sixth president of the U.S. and son of second president John Adams, is born in Braintree, Massachusetts. Andrew Jackson, seventh president of the U.S., is born in Waxhaw settlement, South Carolina.

1769—Daniel Boone sights the Kentucky Territory.

1770—In the Boston Massacre, British soldiers kill five colonists and injure six. Townshend Acts are repealed, thus eliminating all duties on imports to the colonies except tea.

1771—Benjamin Franklin begins his autobiography, a work that he will never complete. The North Carolina assembly passes the "Bloody Act," which makes rioters guilty of treason.

1772—Samuel Adams rouses colonists to consider British threats to self-government. Thomas Jefferson marries Martha Wayles Skelton.

1773—English Parliament passes the Tea Act. Colonists dressed as Mohawk Indians board British tea ships and toss 342 casks of tea into the water in what becomes known as the Boston Tea Party. William Henry Harrison is born in Charles City County, Virginia.

1774—British close the port of Boston to punish the city for the Boston Tea Party. First Continental Congress convenes in Philadelphia.

1775—American Revolution begins with battles of Lexington and Concord, Massachusetts. Second Continental Congress opens in Philadelphia. George Washington becomes commander-in-chief of the Continental army.

1776—Declaration of Independence is adopted on July 4.

1777—Congress adopts the American flag with thirteen stars and thirteen stripes. John Adams is sent to France to negotiate peace treaty.

1778—France declares war against Great Britain and becomes U.S. ally.

1779—British surrender to Americans at Vincennes. Thomas Jefferson is elected governor of Virginia. James Madison is elected to the Continental Congress.

1780—Benedict Arnold, first American traitor, defects to the British.

1781—Articles of Confederation go into effect. Cornwallis surrenders to George Washington at Yorktown, ending the American Revolution.

1782—American commissioners, including John Adams, sign peace treaty with British in Paris. Thomas Jefferson's wife, Martha, dies. Martin Van Buren is born in Kinderhook, New York.

1784—Zachary Taylor is born near Barboursville, Virginia.

1785—Congress adopts the dollar as the unit of currency. John Adams is made minister to Great Britain. Thomas Jefferson is appointed minister to France.

1786—Shays' Rebellion begins in Massachusetts.

1787—Constitutional Convention assembles in Philadelphia, with George Washington presiding; U.S. Constitution is adopted. Delaware, New Jersey, and Pennsylvania become states.

1788—Virginia, South Carolina, New York, Connecticut, New Hampshire, Maryland, and Massachusetts become states. U.S. Constitution is ratified. New York City is declared U.S. capital.

1789—Presidential electors elect George Washington and John Adams as first president and vice-president. Thomas Jefferson is appointed secretary of state. North Carolina becomes a state. French Revolution begins.

1790—Supreme Court meets for the first time. Rhode Island becomes a state. First national census in the U.S. counts 3,929,214 persons. John Tyler is born in Charles City County, Virginia.

1791—Vermont enters the Union. U.S. Bill of Rights, the first ten amendments to the Constitution, goes into effect. District of Columbia is established.

1792—Thomas Paine publishes *The Rights of Man*. Kentucky becomes a state. Two political parties are formed in the U.S., Federalist and Republican. Washington is elected to a second term, with Adams as vice-president.

1793—War between France and Britain begins; U.S. declares neutrality. Eli Whitney invents the cotton gin; cotton production and slave labor increase in the South.

1794—Eleventh Amendment to the Constitution is passed, limiting federal courts' power. "Whiskey Rebellion" in Pennsylvania protests federal whiskey tax. James Madison marries Dolley Payne Todd.

1795—George Washington signs the Jay Treaty with Great Britain. Treaty of San Lorenzo, between U.S. and Spain, settles Florida boundary and gives U.S. right to navigate the Mississippi. James Polk is born near Pineville, North Carolina.

1796—Tennessee enters the Union. Washington gives his Farewell Address, refusing a third presidential term. John Adams is elected president and Thomas Jefferson vice-president.

1797—Adams recommends defense measures against possible war with France. Napoleon Bonaparte and his army march against Austrians in Italy. U.S. population is about 4,900,000.

1798—Washington is named commander-in-chief of the U.S. army. Department of the Navy is created. Alien and Sedition Acts are passed. Napoleon's troops invade Egypt and Switzerland.

1799—George Washington dies at Mount Vernon. James Monroe is elected governor of Virginia. French Revolution ends. Napoleon becomes ruler of France.

1800—Thomas Jefferson and Aaron Burr tie for president. U.S. capital is moved from Philadelphia to Washington, D.C. The White House is built as presidents' home. Spain returns Louisiana to France. Millard Fillmore is born in Locke, New York.

1801—After thirty-six ballots, House of Representatives elects Thomas Jefferson president, making Burr vice-president. James Madison is named secretary of state.

1802—Congress abolishes excise taxes. U.S. Military Academy is founded at West Point, New York.

1803—Ohio enters the Union. Louisiana Purchase treaty is signed with France, greatly expanding U.S. territory.

1804—Twelfth Amendment to the Constitution rules that president and vice-president be elected separately. Alexander Hamilton is killed by Vice-President Aaron Burr in a duel. Orleans Territory is established. Napoleon crowns himself emperor of France.

1805—Thomas Jefferson begins his second term as president. Lewis and Clark expedition reaches the Pacific Ocean.

1806—Coinage of silver dollars is stopped; resumes in 1836.

1807—Aaron Burr is acquitted in treason trial. Embargo Act closes U.S. ports to trade.

1808—James Madison is elected president. Congress outlaws importing slaves from Africa.

1810—U.S. population is 7,240,000.

1811—William Henry Harrison defeats Indians at Tippecanoe. Monroe is named secretary of state.

1812—Louisiana becomes a state. U.S. declares war on Britain (War of 1812). James Madison is reelected president. Napoleon invades Russia.

1813—British forces take Fort Niagara and Buffalo, New York.

1814—Francis Scott Key writes "The Star-Spangled Banner." British troops burn much of Washington, D.C., including the White House. Treaty of Ghent ends War of 1812. James Monroe becomes secretary of war.

1815—Napoleon meets his final defeat at Battle of Waterloo.

1816—James Monroe is elected president. Indiana becomes a state.

1817—Mississippi becomes a state. Construction on Erie Canal begins.

1818—Illinois enters the Union. The present thirteen-stripe flag is adopted. Border between U.S. and Canada is agreed upon.

1819—Alabama becomes a state. U.S. purchases Florida from Spain. Thomas Jefferson establishes the University of Virginia.

1820—James Monroe is reelected. In the Missouri Compromise, Maine enters the Union as a free (non-slave) state.

1821—Missouri enters the Union as a slave state. Santa Fe Trail opens the American Southwest. Mexico declares independence from Spain. Napoleon Bonaparte dies.

1822—U.S. recognizes Mexico and Colombia. Liberia in Africa is founded as a home for freed slaves.

1823—Monroe Doctrine closes North and South America to European colonizing or invasion.

1824—House of Representatives elects John Quincy Adams president when none of the four candidates wins a majority in national election. Mexico becomes a republic.

1825—Erie Canal is opened. U.S. population is 11,300,000.

1826—Thomas Jefferson and John Adams both die on July 4, the fiftieth anniversary of the Declaration of Independence.

1828—Andrew Jackson is elected president. Tariff of Abominations is passed, cutting imports.

1829—James Madison attends Virginia's constitutional convention. Slavery is abolished in Mexico.

1830—Indian Removal Act to resettle Indians west of the Mississippi is approved.

1831—James Monroe dies in New York City. James A. Garfield is born in Orange, Ohio. Cyrus McCormick develops his reaper.

1832—Andrew Jackson, nominated by the new Democratic Party, is reelected president.

1833—Britain abolishes slavery in its colonies.

1835—Federal government becomes debt-free for the first time.

1836—Martin Van Buren becomes president. Texas wins independence from Mexico. Arkansas joins the Union. James Madison dies at Montpelier, Virginia.

1837—Michigan enters the Union. U.S. population is 15,900,000.

1840—William Henry Harrison is elected president.

1841—President Harrison dies in Washington, D.C., one month after inauguration. Vice-President John Tyler succeeds him.

1844—James Knox Polk is elected president. Samuel Morse sends first telegraphic message.

1845—Texas and Florida become states. Potato famine in Ireland causes massive emigration from Ireland to U.S. Andrew Jackson dies near Nashville, Tennessee.

1846—Iowa enters the Union. War with Mexico begins.

1847—U.S. captures Mexico City.

1848—Zachary Taylor becomes president. Treaty of Guadalupe Hidalgo ends Mexico-U.S. war. Wisconsin becomes a state.

1849—James Polk dies in Nashville, Tennessee.

1850—President Taylor dies in Washington, D.C.; Vice-President Millard Fillmore succeeds him. California enters the Union, breaking tie between slave and free states.

1852—Franklin Pierce is elected president.

1853—Gadsden Purchase transfers Mexican territory to U.S.

1854—"War for Bleeding Kansas" is fought between slave and free states.

1855—Czar Nicholas I of Russia dies, succeeded by Alexander II.

1856—James Buchanan is elected president. In Massacre of Potawatomi Creek, Kansas-slavers are murdered by free-staters.

1858 — Minnesota enters the Union. Theodore Roosevelt is born in New York City.

1859 — Oregon becomes a state.

1860 — Abraham Lincoln is elected president; South Carolina secedes from the Union in protest.

1861 — Arkansas, Tennessee, North Carolina, and Virginia secede. Kansas enters the Union as a free state. Civil War begins.

1862 — Union forces capture Fort Henry, Roanoke Island, Fort Donelson, Jacksonville, and New Orleans; Union armies are defeated at the battles of Bull Run and Fredericksburg. Martin Van Buren dies in Kinderhook, New York. John Tyler dies near Charles City, Virginia.

1863 — Lincoln issues Emancipation Proclamation: all slaves held in rebelling territories are declared free. West Virginia becomes a state.

1864 — Abraham Lincoln is reelected. Nevada becomes a state.

1865 — Lincoln is assassinated, succeeded by Andrew Johnson. U.S. Civil War ends on May 26. Thirteenth Amendment abolishes slavery.

1867 — Nebraska becomes a state. U.S. buys Alaska from Russia for $7,200,000. Reconstruction Acts are passed.

1868 — President Johnson is impeached for violating Tenure of Office Act, but is acquitted by Senate. Ulysses S. Grant is elected president. Fourteenth Amendment prohibits voting discrimination.

1870 — Fifteenth Amendment gives blacks the right to vote.

1872 — Grant is reelected over Horace Greeley. General Amnesty Act pardons ex-Confederates.

1874 — Millard Fillmore dies in Buffalo, New York. Herbert Hoover is born in West Branch, Iowa.

1876 — Colorado enters the Union. "Custer's last stand": he and his men are massacred by Sioux Indians at Little Big Horn, Montana.

1877 — Rutherford B. Hayes is elected president as all disputed votes are awarded to him.

1880 — James A. Garfield is elected president.

1881 — President Garfield is assassinated and dies in Elberon, New Jersey. Vice-President Chester A. Arthur succeeds him.

1882 — U.S. bans Chinese immigration. Franklin D. Roosevelt is born in Hyde Park, New York.

1886 — Statue of Liberty is dedicated.

1888 — Benjamin Harrison is elected president.

1889 — North Dakota, South Dakota, Washington, and Montana become states.

1890 — Dwight D. Eisenhower is born in Denison, Texas. Idaho and Wyoming become states.

1892 — Grover Cleveland is elected president.

1896 — William McKinley is elected president. Utah becomes a state.

1898 — U.S. declares war on Spain over Cuba.

1899 — Philippines demand independence from U.S.

1900 — McKinley is reelected. Boxer Rebellion against foreigners in China begins.

1901 — McKinley is assassinated by anarchist; he is succeeded by Theodore Roosevelt.

1902 — U.S. acquires perpetual control over Panama Canal.

1903 — Alaskan frontier is settled.

1904 — Russian-Japanese War breaks out. Theodore Roosevelt wins presidential election.

1905 — Treaty of Portsmouth signed, ending Russian-Japanese War.

1906 — U.S. troops occupy Cuba.

1907 — President Roosevelt bars all Japanese immigration. Oklahoma enters the Union.

1908 — William Howard Taft becomes president. Lyndon B. Johnson is born near Stonewall, Texas.

1909—NAACP is founded under W.E.B. DuBois

1910—China abolishes slavery.

1911—Chinese Revolution begins.

1912—Woodrow Wilson is elected president. Arizona and New Mexico become states.

1913—Federal income tax is introduced in U.S. through the Sixteenth Amendment. Richard Nixon is born in Yorba Linda, California.

1914—World War I begins.

1915—British liner *Lusitania* is sunk by German submarine.

1916—Wilson is reelected president.

1917—U.S. breaks diplomatic relations with Germany. Czar Nicholas of Russia abdicates as revolution begins. U.S. declares war on Austria-Hungary. John F. Kennedy is born in Brookline, Massachusetts.

1918—Wilson proclaims "Fourteen Points" as war aims. On November 11, armistice is signed between Allies and Germany.

1919—Eighteenth Amendment prohibits sale and manufacture of intoxicating liquors. Wilson presides over first League of Nations; wins Nobel Peace Prize. Theodore Roosevelt dies in Oyster Bay, New York.

1920—Nineteenth Amendment (women's suffrage) is passed. Warren Harding is elected president.

1921—Adolf Hitler's stormtroopers begin to terrorize political opponents.

1922—Irish Free State is established. Soviet states form USSR. Benito Mussolini forms Fascist government in Italy.

1923—President Harding dies; he is succeeded by Vice-President Calvin Coolidge.

1924—Coolidge is elected president.

1925—Hitler reorganizes Nazi Party and publishes first volume of *Mein Kampf.*

1926—Fascist youth organizations founded in Germany and Italy. Republic of Lebanon proclaimed.

1927—Stalin becomes Soviet dictator. Economic conference in Geneva attended by fifty-two nations.

1928—Herbert Hoover is elected president. U.S. and many other nations sign Kellogg-Briand pacts to outlaw war.

1929—Stock prices in New York crash on "Black Thursday"; the Great Depression begins.

1930—Bank of U.S. and its many branches close (most significant bank failure of the year).

1931—Emigration from U.S. exceeds immigration for first time as Depression deepens.

1932—Franklin D. Roosevelt wins presidential election in a Democratic landslide.

1933—First concentration camps are erected in Germany. U.S. recognizes USSR and resumes trade. Twenty-First Amendment repeals prohibition.

1934—Severe dust storms hit Plains states. President Roosevelt passes U.S. Social Security Act.

1936—Roosevelt is reelected. Spanish Civil War begins. Hitler and Mussolini form Rome-Berlin Axis.

1937—Roosevelt signs Neutrality Act.

1938—Roosevelt sends appeal to Hitler and Mussolini to settle European problems amicably.

1939—Germany takes over Czechoslovakia and invades Poland, starting World War II.

1940—Roosevelt is reelected for a third term.

1941—Japan bombs Pearl Harbor. U.S. declares war on Japan. Germany and Italy declare war on U.S.; U.S. then declares war on them.

1942—Allies agree not to make separate peace treaties with the enemies. U.S. government transfers more than 100,000 Nisei (Japanese-Americans) from west coast to inland concentration camps.

1943—Allied bombings of Germany begin.

1944—Roosevelt is reelected for a fourth term. Allied forces invade Normandy on D-Day.

1945—President Franklin D. Roosevelt dies in Warm Springs, Georgia; Vice-President Harry S. Truman succeeds him. Mussolini is killed; Hitler commits suicide. Germany surrenders. U.S. drops atomic bomb on Hiroshima; Japan surrenders; end of World War II.

1946—U.N. General Assembly holds its first session in London. Peace conference of twenty-one nations is held in Paris.

1947—Peace treaties are signed in Paris. "Cold War" is in full swing.

1948—U.S. passes Marshall Plan Act, providing $17 billion in aid for Europe. U.S. recognizes new nation of Israel. India and Pakistan become free of British rule. Truman is elected president.

1949—Republic of Eire is proclaimed in Dublin. Russia blocks land route access from Western Germany to Berlin; airlift begins. U.S., France, and Britain agree to merge their zones of occupation in West Germany. Apartheid program begins in South Africa.

1950—Riots in Johannesburg, South Africa, against apartheid. North Korea invades South Korea. U.N. forces land in South Korea and recapture Seoul.

1951—Twenty-Second Amendment limits president to two terms.

1952—Dwight D. Eisenhower resigns as supreme commander in Europe and is elected president.

1953—Stalin dies; struggle for power in Russia follows. Rosenbergs are executed for espionage.

1954—U.S. and Japan sign mutual defense agreement.

1955—Blacks in Montgomery, Alabama, boycott segregated bus lines.

1956—Eisenhower is reelected president. Soviet troops march into Hungary.

1957—U.S. agrees to withdraw ground forces from Japan. Russia launches first satellite, *Sputnik.*

1958—European Common Market comes into being. Alaska becomes the forty-ninth state. Fidel Castro begins war against Batista government in Cuba.

1959—Hawaii becomes fiftieth state. Castro becomes premier of Cuba. De Gaulle is proclaimed president of the Fifth Republic of France.

1960—Historic debates between Senator John F. Kennedy and Vice-President Richard Nixon are televised. Kennedy is elected president. Brezhnev becomes president of USSR.

1961—Berlin Wall is constructed. Kennedy and Khrushchev confer in Vienna. In Bay of Pigs incident, Cubans trained by CIA attempt to overthrow Castro.

1962—U.S. military council is established in South Vietnam.

1963—Riots and beatings by police and whites mark civil rights demonstrations in Birmingham, Alabama; 30,000 troops are called out. Martin Luther King, Jr., is arrested. Freedom marchers descend on Washington, D.C., to demonstrate. President Kennedy is assassinated in Dallas, Texas; Vice-President Lyndon B. Johnson is sworn in as president.

1964—U.S. aircraft bomb North Vietnam. Johnson is elected president. Herbert Hoover dies in New York City.

1965—U.S. combat troops arrive in South Vietnam.

1966—Thousands protest U.S. policy in Vietnam. National Guard quells race riots in Chicago.

1967—Six-Day War between Israel and Arab nations.

1968—Martin Luther King, Jr., is assassinated in Memphis, Tennessee. Senator Robert Kennedy is assassinated in Los Angeles. Riots and police brutality take place at Democratic National Convention in Chicago. Richard Nixon is elected president. Czechoslovakia is invaded by Soviet troops.

1969—Dwight D. Eisenhower dies in Washington, D.C. Hundreds of thousands of people in several U.S. cities demonstrate against Vietnam War.

1970—Four Vietnam War protesters are killed by National Guardsmen at Kent State University in Ohio.

1971—Twenty-Sixth Amendment allows eighteen-year-olds to vote.

1972—Nixon visits Communist China; is reelected president in near-record landslide. Watergate affair begins when five men are arrested in the Watergate hotel complex in Washington, D.C. Nixon announces resignations of aides Haldeman, Ehrlichman, and Dean and Attorney General Kleindienst as a result of Watergate-related charges. Harry S. Truman dies in Kansas City, Missouri.

1973—Vice-President Spiro Agnew resigns; Gerald Ford is named vice-president. Vietnam peace treaty is formally approved after nineteen months of negotiations. Lyndon B. Johnson dies in San Antonio, Texas.

1974—As a result of Watergate cover-up, impeachment is considered; Nixon resigns and Ford becomes president. Ford pardons Nixon and grants limited amnesty to Vietnam War draft evaders and military deserters.

1975—U.S. civilians are evacuated from Saigon, South Vietnam, as Communist forces complete takeover of South Vietnam.

1976—U.S. celebrates its Bicentennial. James Earl Carter becomes president.

1977—Carter pardons most Vietnam draft evaders, numbering some 10,000.

1980—Ronald Reagan is elected president.

1981—President Reagan is shot in the chest in assassination attempt. Sandra Day O'Connor is appointed first woman justice of the Supreme Court.

1983—U.S. troops invade island of Grenada.

1984—Reagan is reelected president. Democratic candidate Walter Mondale's running mate, Geraldine Ferraro, is the first woman selected for vice-president by a major U.S. political party.

1985—Soviet Communist Party secretary Konstantin Chernenko dies; Mikhail Gorbachev succeeds him. U.S. and Soviet officials discuss arms control in Geneva. Reagan and Gorbachev hold summit conference in Geneva. Racial tensions accelerate in South Africa.

1986—Space shuttle *Challenger* explodes shortly after takeoff; crew of seven dies. U.S. bombs bases in Libya. Corazon Aquino defeats Ferdinand Marcos in Philippine presidential election.

1987—Iraqi missile rips the U.S. frigate *Stark* in the Persian Gulf, killing thirty-seven American sailors. Congress holds hearings to investigate sale of U.S. arms to Iran to finance Nicaraguan *contra* movement.

Index

Page numbers in boldface type indicate illustrations.

About the Author

Zachary Kent grew up in Little Falls, New Jersey, and received an English degree from St. Lawrence University. Following college he worked at a New York City literary agency for two years and then launched his writing career. To support himself while writing, he has worked as a taxi driver, a shipping clerk, and a house painter. Mr. Kent has had a lifelong interest in American history. Studying the U.S. presidents was his childhood hobby. His collection of presidential items includes books, pictures, and games, as well as several autographed letters.